Katie
LET'S CELEBRATE YOUR STORY

SPREAD YOUR WINGS

A SELF-DISCOVERY JOURNAL

sourcebooks
eXplore

TO MAUREEN AND TOM.
FROM MY FIRST WOBBLY STEPS
UNTIL THAT MOMENT WHEN THERE
WAS NO SOIL BENEATH MY FEET:
YOU ALWAYS KNEW I'D FIND MY WINGS.

NIKLAS'S ART.
AGE 5

Published by Sourcebooks eXplore, an imprint of Sourcebooks Kids
P.O. Box 4410, Naperville, Illinois 60567–4410
(630) 961-3900
sourcebookskids.com

Source of Production: Versa Press, East Peoria, Illinois, USA
Date of Production: January 2020
Run Number: 5017014

Printed and bound in the United States of America.
VP 10 9 8 7 6 5 4 3 2 1

ON TAKING FLIGHT

I WAS AMAZED BY HOW PEACEFUL the summer morning appeared, because that's not how I was feeling. I was sitting in a 1950s four-seat airplane, alone. The engine roared, but it could not drown out my banging heart as I taxied to the runway.

For years, I'd been amassing a cozy cage around myself, monologuing about how I could never be a pilot. I argued that my poor grasp of physics, mechanics, and aerodynamics made it impossible; my struggles with motion sickness made it uncomfortable; and the waste of precious time and money made it impractical. My subconscious had convinced me that my life was better if I kept saying "I can't" rather than face my fear and try.

Self-doubt keeps us grounded. It knows we don't like that uncomfortable feeling of uncertainty, so it reminds us that we're much safer when we fold up our big, beautiful wings and ignore possibility. Nothing will upset our pride, our wallets, our relationships—our comfort zone—if we remain where we are and never attempt to soar.

But I've also discovered that we learn the most about ourselves when we seek things we never imagined we could do. So on that warm Montana morning, I took my first solo flight.

"You've got this, Katie!" I coached myself as I engaged the throttle. My little Cessna catapulted across the runway and into the sky. I was sweating. But as the plane climbed rapidly without the weight of my instructor, the view of the world became more beautiful than I'd ever imagined, and I relaxed. I knew I'd return to the ground a stronger, braver version of myself.

Earlier that year, I had journaled my desire to earn a private pilot's license. I've always enjoyed journaling because it grants me access to the birdsong in my heart—that inner voice of truth. And I delight in witnessing how it does that for others. Journals offer us space to navigate away from the chaos of life so we can lean into who we are and examine our flight plans. In a world where it's increasingly easy to get sidetracked by what we perceive others think, pausing for a few moments to journal gives us the opportunity to reflect on our unique experiences, acknowledge our emotions, and honestly plan our future. Even the briefest entries can help cast off self-doubt and unlock the cage we've unknowingly built around ourselves, and can reveal beauty and confidence where we didn't know it existed.

The more I journaled about why I wanted to fly, the more I jumped into the cockpit. When I started taking lessons, journaling is what got me through many tears of frustration, aborted landings, and moments when I had to completely surrender control of the aircraft to my instructor. Slowly, my tears of frustration metamorphosed into tears of joy. I felt freer and braver.

As I soloed across the sky, I adjusted levers and dials like they were pieces of me. I radioed my intentions for the world to hear, and then shifted from rising in the sky to descending back to the ground. My wings were stretched; I loved how it felt.

This journal is my invitation to help you navigate to a more joyful, fulfilled version of yourself. These pages will guide you to recognize your roots, relish opportunities, and help transform dreams to reality. Some questions might make you laugh, while others might feel uncomfortable to confront, though I believe they'll all ultimately bring you closer to discovering your true self. Keep these four guideposts in mind as you begin your journey of discovery.

1. ABANDON PERFECTION.

Life is messy, yet we tell ourselves that a journal about our lives can't contain chaos. I have found that jotting down some story is infinitely better than writing nothing, so take a deep breath and toss perfectionism out. Fill this time capsule with your moments of gratitude, courage, and self-exploration. Allow yourself to address occasional topics that may feel awkward or painful. These reflections will ultimately make your life richer.

I cross out sentences, make bumbling grammar mistakes, and invent new vocabulary in my entries all the time. If you try to preemptively outline ideas or edit as you go, you unintentionally lose most of the raw truth and best revelations that arise from letting your pen and heart wander across the page. So flip your journal open to any prompt, then set a timer and write until it dings. Or imagine you're holding an intimate conversation with your innermost self.

2. WRITE WITH SELF-LOVE.

The journey to really trusting who you are isn't always easy. You'll encounter moments that require you to face fear, claim your strength, and sometimes forgive. (I know how scary it is to accept things you can't control or stand when you feel vulnerable.) This journal is your personal love letter. Use it to nurture yourself as you write, to reflect and embrace ideas that are uniquely yours. I believe that as you fill these pages with words of self-kindness, you'll unearth genuine confidence and joy.

3. PLAY.

This journal is a home for words; it's also your place to play! Doodle and sketch. Paint. Collage. Use your childhood stickers or shop for more. Experiment with pens and penmanship. Add photographs, screenshots, and mementos. Above all, have fun. The playful process of gathering keepsakes and embellishing your journal gives you an opportunity to further reflect on ideas you've written and express yourself in different ways.

4. TAKE FLIGHT.

As you begin writing, come watch my TEDxTalk at katieclemons.com. It's a timely segue into exploring self-love, confronting vulnerability, and discovering strength in your story.

You're also warmly welcome to explore my exclusive *Spread Your Wings* printables, good reads, and Saturday-night-in self-care recommendations. And take a peek in my journals, too:

KATIECLEMONS.COM/A/E5A1

I'd love to hear how you're stretching your wings in your own special way! Drop me a note at **howdy@katieclemons.com** (I answer all my mail) or join me on social media **@katierclemons**, **#katieclemonsjournals**, and **#spreadyourwingsjournal**.

You were born to fly. Spread your wings, and... Let's celebrate your story!

LET'S START HERE.

My full name is

_____

I usually go by

_____

Three words that describe me are

1.

2.

3.

I'm _____ years old, which is a fabulous age because

_____

_____

_____

_____

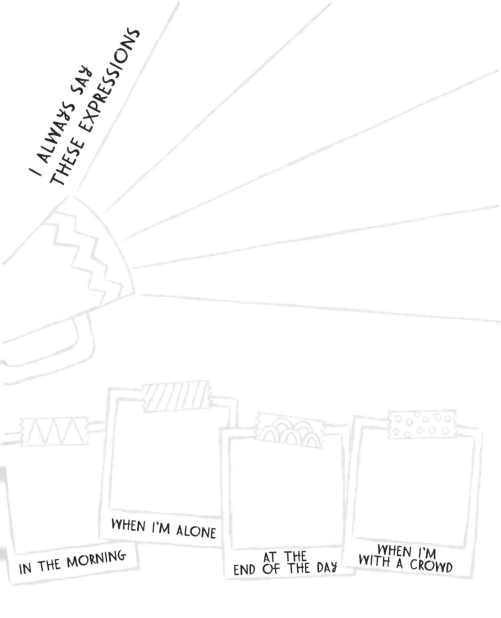

I ALWAYS SAY THESE EXPRESSIONS

WHEN I'M ALONE

IN THE MORNING

AT THE END OF THE DAY

WHEN I'M WITH A CROWD

TODAY I START SPREADING MY WINGS!

DATE: _____

MY JOURNAL
GUIDELINES

1. My top focus(es) in this journal will be to

☐ Express my thoughts

☐ Use perfect grammar

☐ Let go of perfection and enjoy the process

☐ Write what I think and feel and not what I perceive
other people want

☐ Create a snapshot of my life right now

☐ ....

☐ ....

2. What are my thoughts on these? ....

....

....

3. Why is keeping this journal important to me?
Is there something I want to unearth about myself?

....

....

....

4. Is there a specific date when this journal must be complete? _____

5. How consistently do I need to write to make that happen?

_____

_____

6. Should I complete the pages of this journal in numerical order?   ☐ YES   ☐ NO

7. What could I do if I need more space to write?

_____

_____

8. Am I comfortable with anyone else looking inside these pages? Who? _____

_____

9. How would I like to celebrate the completion of this journal? _____

_____

10. Are there any other guidelines I'd like to establish before I dive in? _____

_____

HERE'S A CURRENT PHOTOGRAPH OR DRAWING OF ME.

When I look at this picture, I feel

Two of my best traits that this picture shows

1.

2.

Two great traits it doesn't reveal

1.

2.

HERE'S A PHOTOGRAPH OR DRAWING
OF WHAT I HOPE TO BE
IN _____ YEARS.

When I look at this picture, I feel

I really want this because

In order to get there, I know I need

A TWO-PAGE
MEMOIR

Who I am and astonishing things I've done!

CURRENTLY ON MY

bedroom walls

bucket list

mind

playlist

breakfast plate

to do list

feet

nightstand

bathroom
sink

wish list

bed

dinner plate

I LIKE TO

TASTE   HEAR

WATCH   FEEL

BEGIN   SMELL

FINISH   RELAX WITH

I DON'T LIKE TO

TASTE

HEAR

WATCH

FEEL

BEGIN

SMELL

FINISH

RELAX WITH

ONE DAY, I'D LIKE TO

TASTE

☐ Completed on:

HEAR

☐ Completed on:

WATCH

☐ Completed on:

FEEL

☐ Completed on:

BEGIN

☐ Completed on:

SMELL

☐ Completed on:

FINISH

☐ Completed on:

RELAX WITH

☐ Completed on:

DATE

I'M SO GRATEFUL FOR

1.
2.
3.
4.
5.

THIS IS HOW I TAKE CARE OF MYSELF

HERE'S A DRAWING, PICTURE, OR RECENT MEMENTO

25

THREE THINGS

My days are filled with

1.

2.

3.

I always have time for

1.

2.

3.

I never have time for

1.

2.

3.

MY TYPICAL DAY

5:00

6:00

7:00

8:00

9:00

10:00

11:00

NOON

1:00

2:00

3:00

4:00

5:00

6:00

7:00

8:00

9:00

10:00

11:00

MIDNIGHT

A FEW OF MY
FAVORITE THINGS

KIND OF VACATION

ICE CREAM FLAVOR

GO-TO SHIRT

CANDY

WILD ANIMAL

COLOR

28

HOLIDAY

SONG

WEBSITE

SPOT AT HOME

EVERYDAY SHOES

MORNING DRINK

29

AROUND HERE

I'm really happy that

I'm ashamed of

I'm wondering when

I'm confident I can

I'm jealous of

I appreciate

I adore

I'm overwhelmed by

I'm hopeful that

THREE THINGS

I'm undoubtedly great at

1.

2.

3.

I'm really proud of myself for

1.

2.

3.

I'm glad I got to experience

1.

2.

3.

DATE

HERE'S AN INSPIRING QUOTATION, PASSAGE, OR POEM I LOVE

I'M ADDING IT TO MY JOURNAL BECAUSE

33

DATE

8 THINGS
THAT ALWAYS MAKE ME
HAPPY

34

TO ME, SUCCESS MEANS

WAYS I'VE ALREADY FOUND
HAPPINESS OR SUCCESS

I KNOW I'M LUCKY BECAUSE

39

AROUND HERE

I'm getting excited about
_____

_____

_____

I'm curious about
_____

_____

_____

I feel guilty that
_____

_____

_____

I feel lonely when
_____

_____

_____

I'm angry about

I'm worried because

I'm grateful for

I can't understand how

I'm wondering when

PASSIONATE PEOPLE

 INSPIRES ME BECAUSE

I HOPE I EMULATE THIS PERSON WHEN

I STRIVE TO BE MORE LIKE THIS PERSON BY

_____ INSPIRES ME BECAUSE

I HOPE I EMULATE THIS PERSON WHEN

I STRIVE TO BE MORE LIKE THIS PERSON BY

INSPIRES ME BECAUSE

I HOPE I EMULATE THIS PERSON WHEN

I STRIVE TO BE MORE LIKE THIS PERSON BY

INSPIRES ME BECAUSE

I HOPE I EMULATE THIS PERSON WHEN

I STRIVE TO BE MORE LIKE THIS PERSON BY

THINGS THAT CURRENTLY FRUSTRATE ME ABOUT MYSELF AND WHY

THINGS I CAN DO ABOUT IT, WHETHER THAT'S ACCEPTANCE OR CHANGE

TRENDS AND INTERESTING
REVELATIONS ABOUT MYSELF

RECENT MOMENTS WHEN I'VE FELT

COURAGEOUS

COMPOSED

CONFIDENT

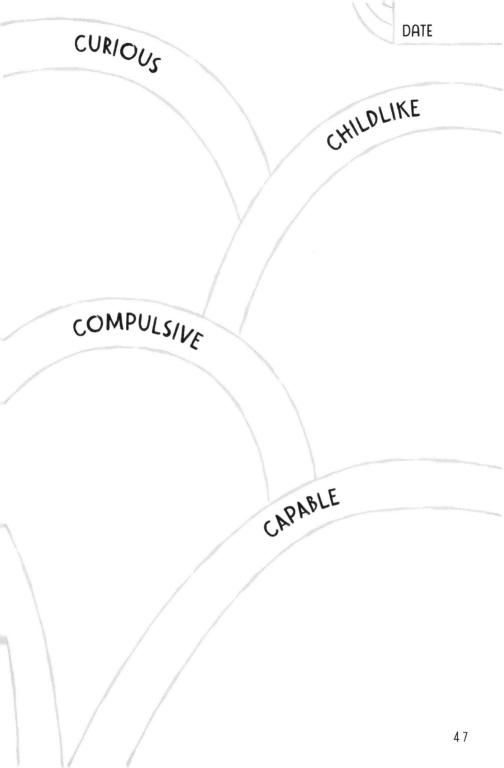

CURIOUS

CHILDLIKE

COMPULSIVE

CAPABLE

WHEN I WAS YOUNGER

I won an award for

I think it's reflective of who I am today because

HOBBIES AND
ACTIVITIES
I LOVED WHEN
I WAS YOUNGER

WHEN I WAS YOUNGER

My best school subjects were

When I was uninterrupted at home, I liked to spend my time

I accumulated a lot of

I dreamed of trying all these jobs or careers

COMPLIMENTS I RECEIVED ABOUT MY
TALENTS OR PERSONALITY
WHEN I WAS YOUNGER

I LOVE THESE
CHILDHOOD MEMORIES

THREE THINGS

I kept from childhood

1.

2.

3.

I wish I still had from childhood

1.

2.

3.

I'll never forget about my childhood bedroom

1.

2.

3.

I don't do enough of anymore

1.

2.

3.

I used to do (and would do again)

1.

2.

3.

I'd like to try for the first time

1.

2.

3.

I'VE ALREADY CLIMBED SO FAR!

This is my victory log of my favorite experiences,
achievements, and dreams come true.

BIRTH DATE:

TODAY'S DATE:

Keep this log in your journal or hang it
up to celebrate how far you've come.

I GIVE MYSELF PERMISSION

TO SAY YES TO

TO SAY NO TO

TO PUT MYSELF FIRST WHEN

TO FORGIVE MYSELF FOR

TIMES WHEN I HAVE FELT

peace

hurt

belonging

vulnerability

humiliation

surprise

curiosity

worry

WHAT IF I STARTED INVESTING IN TWO OF THESE THINGS RIGHT NOW?

ONE FOR ME

ONE FOR OTHERS

WHAT'S STOPPING ME?

FAILURE

I'M AFRAID TO FAIL BECAUSE

DATE

HERE'S AN EXAMPLE OF WHEN I FELT
LIKE I'D FAILED

THAT EXPERIENCE MADE ME FEEL

TODAY I'M ☐ STILL BOTHERED BY IT
☐ NOT BOTHERED BY IT BECAUSE

HOW COULD I LOOK AT FAILURE AS A
GOOD THING?

BEAUTIFUL AND BRAVE THINGS
THAT PAST GENERATIONS OF
MY FAMILY HAVE DONE

I NEVER THOUGHT THAT I'D BE ABLE TO

AND THEN I DID IT!

SOMETIMES
I FEEL LIKE I HAVE TO
HIDE MY TRUE SELF
BECAUSE

What I think others want to see

What I want to reveal

TODAY I AM

ENJOYING

HOPING

FEELING

ANTICIPATING

THANKING

COORDINATING

SMELLING

DREADING

WISHING

UNDERSTANDING

AROUND HERE I COULD

Be kinder to myself by _____

_____

_____

_____

Forgive myself for _____

_____

_____

_____

Bring more laughter or serenity to my days by

_____

_____

_____

_____

Let go of possessions that don't bring me happiness
such as _____

_____

_____

_____

Discontinue commitments and activities that don't
enable me to live the life I want such as

Strengthen the most important relationships in my life by

Express gratitude to people and organizations that
nurture me by

I want to invest in these subtle changes for myself because

AROUND HERE I WILL

Start charging my batteries by

Make more time for

Say NO to

Pay more attention to

Finally begin to

AROUND HERE I WANT

To have

To achieve

To see

To let go of

To know how to

THIS IS ME

I can sing every word of

I own my own

I collect

I'm not afraid of

For lunch, I like

I'm really proud of myself because today I

When no one's looking, I can eat an entire

I can't decide if

Most nights, I remember to

I'm not worried about

But I am worried about

I wish people cared more about

When I was younger, I had a reputation of being

It ☐ was ☐ wasn't a fair assumption because

I could binge read

I have binge read

ACCOMPLISHMENTS FROM THE PAST YEAR THAT I'M PROUD OF

Defining moments and people that helped make my achievements happen

▷

▷

▷

How I celebrated or acknowledged each victory

▷

▷

▷

Ways I still need to honor what I've done

▷

▷

▷

HERE'S A RECENT
PICTURE OF ME

Looking at this picture makes me feel

_____

_____

_____

_____

_____

I think it captures a part of my true self because

_____

_____

_____

_____

_____

I feel like I radiate beauty in this picture because

_____

_____

_____

_____

_____

ACCOMPLISHMENTS FROM THE PAST _____ YEARS THAT I'M PROUD OF

Defining moments and people that helped make my achievements happen

▷

▷

▷

How I celebrated or acknowledged each victory

▷

▷

▷

Ways I still need to honor what I've done

▷

▷

▷

I WANT TO HAVE

TIME FOR

A HOME THAT

A BODY THAT

A FAMILY THAT

ENOUGH MONEY TO

NEIGHBORS AND FRIENDS WHO

THE COURAGE TO

A LIFE THAT'S

I'M FORTUNATE
TO ALREADY HAVE

TIME FOR

A HOME THAT

A BODY THAT

A FAMILY THAT

ENOUGH MONEY TO

NEIGHBORS AND FRIENDS WHO

THE COURAGE TO

A LIFE THAT'S

WHAT'S MISSING BETWEEN WHAT I HAVE AND WHAT I DESIRE?

WHEN I SILENCE THE NOISE, I CAN
HEAR MY HEART TELLING ME

DEAR HEAD,

It's okay to let go of

DEAR HEART,

It's okay to let go of

THINGS THAT CURRENTLY CAUSE ME STRESS

THINGS THAT CURRENTLY BRING ME JOY

THE 3 THINGS I COVET
MORE THAN ANYTHING IN MY LIFE

THEY'RE IMPORTANT TO ME BECAUSE

I GIVE MYSELF PERMISSION

TO CRY WHEN

TO STAND UP FOR MYSELF WHEN

TO LOVE MYSELF WHEN

TO KEEP GOING WHEN

THESE ARE WAYS
I CAN START NURTURING
MY DREAMS

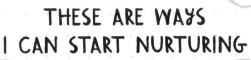

TODAY I AM

HESITATING

NEEDING

WANTING

GIVING

IGNORING

TRYING

TASTING

ORGANIZING

PRACTICING

BELIEVING

I AM ENOUGH
HERE ARE THE REASONS WHY

5 WAYS I SHOW
KINDNESS AND GRATITUDE

To myself

1.
2.
3.
4.
5.

To others

1.
2.
3.
4.
5.

THIS IS MY

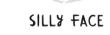

SILLY FACE

CRABBY FACE

LATE-FOR-SOMETHING FACE

PROUD FACE

SLEEPING FACE

CURRENT FACE

THIS IS MY BEDROOM

IT USUALLY LOOKS LIKE

☐ a museum of oddities   ☐ a cleaning commercial

☐ a science experiment   ☐ a tornado hit

☐ a paper explosion   ☐ a gold mine

☐ _____   ☐ _____

MY **COLOSSAL**, POTENTIALLY IMPOSSIBLE LIST OF DREAMS

SO BIG I'M ALMOST AFRAID TO PUT THEM ON THIS PAGE

HOW I CAN MAKE
THESE DREAMS **POSSIBLE**

HERE'S WHAT I KNOW
ABOUT MYSELF

I laugh when _____

_____

I cry when _____

_____

I sing when _____

_____

I dance when _____

_____

I freeze in my tracks when _____

_____

I push myself forward when _____

_____

WHAT WOULD I DO IF I HAD

$100 to spend on myself

$100 to
help other people

100 hours to
develop a new skill

100 hours to help others

IN ONE BIG AND BRAVE SENTENCE,
THIS IS WHAT I REALLY WANT

WHAT KIND OF LIFE WOULD I LIVE IF I WEREN'T AFRAID?

WHAT DOES MY GUT
KEEP TELLING ME?

TIMES WHEN I HAVE FELT

LOVE

FEAR

COMPASSION

ANGER

POWERLESSNESS

BLISS

GRATITUDE

INDIFFERENCE

TIMES WHEN I HAVE FELT

PEACE

HURT

VULNERABILITY

HUMILIATION

BELONGING

SURPRISE

WORRY

CURIOSITY

LOVE ♡ FEAR
COMPASSION
ANGER
POWERLESSNESS
BLISS ☼ GRATITUDE
INDIFFERENCE
PEACE ✿ HURT
VULNERABILITY
HUMILIATION
BELONGING ♡
SURPRISE 💍 WORRY
CURIOSITY

The emotions that were the easiest to describe

I think it's because

The emotions I'd like to experience more are

I want to feel them more because

Little things I could do to bring them into my life include

The emotions I'd like to experience less are

I want to feel them less because

Little things I could do to minimize them in my life include

FEAR

In one word, the thing I'm most fearful of is

To me, that word means

How much is my fear based on what I perceive others might think?

Who are those people? Why do their opinions matter?

How does my fear influence my actions?

What if I never felt that fear and pressure?

What would I do differently?

How could I begin to let go of this fear's control over me?

THESE PEOPLE **SUPPORT** ME AND **CHEER** FOR ME

WHO

1.

2.

3.

4.

5.

DATE

HOW

1.

2.

3.

4.

5.

127

PROBLEMS I'M GOOD
AT SOLVING

1.

2.

3.

4.

5.

MY SKILLS AND TALENTS
THAT HELP

1.

2.

3.

4.

5.

MY CHILDHOOD SELF WOULD BE **PROUD** OF ME TODAY BECAUSE

MY FAVORITE WAY TO SPEND A
SATURDAY MORNING

CHILDHOOD

When I
was alone

With family
or friends

TODAY

When I'm
alone

With family
or friends

GIVING THANKS

DEAR _____,

the person or people who raised me,

I admire you for

I'm grateful that you

DEAR

my favorite childhood teacher,

I admire you for

Thank you for

DEAR

my biggest cheerleader,

I admire you for

Thank you for

HERE'S A PICTURE OF ME STRETCHING MY WINGS!

I KNOW I AM

Worthy of love because

Deserving of respect because

Brave because

Beautiful inside because

Capable because

10 YEARS FROM NOW

What I hope changes in my life

What I hope remains the same

DREAMS FOR MYSELF OVER
THE NEXT _____ YEARS

in love

at work

for fun

I PREDICT IN _____ YEARS

I'll have

I'll have achieved

I'll have seen

I'll have made room in my life for

I'll know how to

DEAR FUTURE ME,

Here's what I want you to know about who I am today

This is what I want from you

I WANT TO KEEP CLIMBING!

This is my wish list of future experiences, achievements, and dreams I want to make come true.

TODAY'S DATE:

FUTURE DATE:

Keep this log in your journal or hang it
up to celebrate how far you've come.

HERE'S ONE LAST
LOVE LETTER TO MYSELF